Reaping the Harvest
of God's Word

Reaping the Harvest of God's Word

A Collection of Inspirational Poems

Donnalee Jemmison

REAPING THE HARVEST OF GOD'S WORD
Copyright © 2016 by Donnalee Jemmison

All rights reserved. Neither this publication nor any part of this publication may be reproduced or transmitted in any form or by any means, electronic or mechanical, including photocopying, recording or any information storage and retrieval system, without permission in writing from the author.

Printed in Canada

ISBN: 978-1-4866-1308-3

Word Alive Press
131 Cordite Road, Winnipeg, MB R3W 1S1
www.wordalivepress.ca

WORD ALIVE
—P R E S S—

MIX
Paper from responsible sources
FSC FSC® C016245

Jemmison, Donnalee, 1981-, author
    Reaping the harvest of God's word : a collection of inspirational poems / Donnalee Jemmison.

Issued in print and electronic formats.
ISBN 978-1-4866-1308-3 (paperback).--ISBN 978-1-4866-1309-0 (ebook)

    1. Christian poetry, Canadian (English). I. Title.

PS8619.E45R43 2016	C811'.6	C2016-901439-8
		C2016-901440-1

Contents

	Introduction	vii
1.	Connected to the Vine	1
2.	Exercise Your Faith	2
3.	I am Taking my Godly Authority	7
4.	Let Us Never Forget for Us He Died	12
5.	Love	15
6.	Peace	18
7.	Prayer of Faith	20
8.	Serve the Lord Today	22
9.	The Almighty God	25
10.	The Year of Release	29
11.	What is My Duty?	33
12.	You Might Be the Only Jesus They See	35
	About the Author	41

Introduction

*Reaping the Harvest of God`s Word* is a riveting collection of poetic artistry that addresses a variety of subject matters contained in God`s Holy scriptures. In this book you will find poetry concerning being connected to God, having faith to believe in the impossible, walking in godly authority, remembering Christ`s passion, love through God`s eyes, peace of mind, effective prayer, serving the Lord, being released from bondages, and the duty and commission of a believer. *Reaping the Harvest of God`s Word* will motivate and influence you in a positive way, improving your moral and spiritual outlook, building you up a spiritual house, founded upon the word of God.

Connected to the Vine

I just want to be connected to the vine
Truly know that God is mine

Through this world of toil, I cannot bear it alone
On Christ the solid rock, my anchor holds

Lord Jesus I want to abide in thee
Make me Jesus a righteous tree

Purged with hyssop and washed in your blood
Engulfed in your presence, filled with your love

May I keep your word hid in my heart
Abiding in you, from your will, I will not depart

From day to day as I run this race
Let your Holy Spirit arise and let self be abase

Make me Jesus what you want me to be
Connected to the vine, I just want to be more like thee
Have your own way, I seek your will divine
I just want to be connected to the vine

Exercise Your Faith

What I declare and decree it shall come to pass
I will see the manifestation of my faith at last

Grow in faith, don't be stagnant or still
Forward still, it is Jehovah's will

Exercise your faith without fear or doubt
Life and death is in the power of what comes out
   of your mouth

When Job's wife told him to curse God and die in
   insulting accusation
Job stood in faith and told his wife she speaks like
   one of the foolish women
All the days of my appointed time will I wait until
   my change comes

Job waited on the Lord and his latter was greater
   than his past
He saw the manifestation of his faith at last

Stand now in faith instead of murmuring and complaining
Say where I am now is not where I am staying

There are greater heights and deeper depths
I'm seeking for my life, God's very best

Now faith is the substance of things hoped for the evidence of things not seen
By faith Enoch was translated for he bared the testimony that with him God was pleased

By faith Abel offered a more excellent sacrifice than Cain
As a result of Cain's jealousy Abel was slain
Yet still Abel's blood cried out from the grave

But without faith it is impossible to please Him
For he that cometh to God must believe that He is
And He is a rewarder of them that diligently seek Him

By faith Noah built an ark in preparation for the flood
He did not see it, but moved in faith upon the word of God

By faith Moses and the children of Israel passed through the Red sea by dry land
Which the Egyptians assaying to do, to their demise they were drowned

Sometimes when you are going through and you can't find peace or rest
Hold on my brother, hold on my sister, it is just a test

For the race is not for the fast nor the swift, but he who can endure
Gods promises are true, Gods promises are sure

By faith when the Lord had shut up her womb, Hanna prayed earnestly
She trusted the Lord and believed for her breakthrough and she was able to conceive

God is not blind to us, He sees our silent tears
He is a God that is faithful and hears and answers prayers

Know who you are and whose you are and go about without a care
Some may even look on and say favor just ain't fair

They did not see when you put the Lord before your face in the midnight hours
How you cried from the abundance of your heart and prayed down God's power

By faith the woman with the issue of blood, who had spent all her living on physicians
Pressed through the crowd and was made immediately whole when she touched the hem of Jesus' garment

It may seem sometimes that you've been waiting so long and you can't see the light of day
Well just press on and press along, your blessing is on its way
Weary and tired, feeling like you've had enough
Speak life into your situation and you shall eat the fruit thereof

The words you say and what you think should not be taken lightly
Bear in mind you are your own self fulfilling prophesy

I would also put you in remembrance and be it made known
That what you are going to reap is that which you've already sown

Be not tossed to and fro with a spirit of wavering
Be steadfast and sure knowing who your savior is

Faith without reservation
Let that be our determination

If you are willing to patiently wait
Then you will see the fulfillment of the end of your faith

I am Taking my Godly Authority

I am taking my Godly authority
I am going to be what God has called me to be

With arms stretched wide, He bled and died
They nailed His hands, they pierced His side

They beat Him and scourged Him and put a crown
  of thorns upon His head too
As they mocked Him, in His compassion He cried,
  "Father, forgive them, for they know not what
  they do"

Jesus sacrificed His life because of love you see
So that we could live and not die for all eternity

He endured such contradiction of sinners
So that you and I would come out winners

He bore our guilt, our pain and our sorrow
And because He lives, I can face tomorrow

He overcame sin, hell, death and the grave
I now have obtained power and authority through Jesus' name

I am taking my Godly authority
I am going to be what God has called me to be

Speaking those things that are not as though they already are
Calling things into being from near and far

I am more than a conqueror, the head and not the tail,
Strong and mighty through God, in every circumstance I prevail

I have the unmerited favor of God on my life
I walk in abundance free from pain and strife

I am the very righteousness of God
Walking in holiness, cleansed by His blood

I am taking my Godly authority
I am going to be what God has called me to be

I am blessed in the city, I am blessed in the field
I am blessed in my going out and in my coming in
I know who I am, royalty, a child of the King

As I'm knocking doors are opening
As I'm seeking I shall find
As I ask it shall be given
Because Jesus is mine

I am like the tree planted by the rivers of water that
   bringeth forth his fruit in due season
The angels of the Lord encampeth round about me
   and are surrounding me in legions

Everything my hand touches prospers and succeeds
As I fast and pray and worship God, on fertile
   ground I am sowing seeds

I walk in generational blessings, every curse is lifted
Every yoke is broken, I am anointed and I am gifted

I am destined for greatness, the Lord is paving my
   way
Victory after victory, new mercies I'm seeing everyday

I am blessed and highly favored, the Lord knows my name
Consecrated unto God, my life will never be the same

I am taking my Godly authority
I am going to be what God has called me to be

As I bind it and loose it on earth, so it is in heaven
Your power and authority is already given

You just have to speak it and unleash it, shifting the atmosphere
And trust in God with all your heart, casting on Him your cares

If I'm sick in my body, despite how I feel
I will boldly declare with His stripes I am healed

Every weapon that is formed against me is brought to naught
He has purchased my salvation, by His shed blood my soul is redeemed and bought

Don't be discouraged, let not your heart be troubled and hold your head up
Remembering the effectual fervent prayer of a righteous man availeth much

I am taking my Godly authority
I am going to be what God has called me to be

Let Us Never Forget for Us He Died

Let us never forget for us He died
Christ our savior crucified
Nailed to the cross with arms stretched wide
His feet were nailed, they pierced His side

In His body He bore our sorrows and our shame
He suffered for our sin, He took the blame
In the midst of the agony He was mindful of me
He was mindful of me amidst the pain

On the cross of Calvary He purchased my destiny
He came that we might have life and have it more
    abundantly

Because of the cross I will live and not die
Because of the cross we are no longer orphans
But now, have received power to be called daugh-
    ters and sons

Of God, who is no fraud
For He is real, yes I know He is real

He died on the cross and rose the third day
He overcame sin, death and the grave
We now have victory through that precious name
Jesus Christ, yesterday, today, forever the same
Remember godliness with contentment it is great gain
And if we suffer with Him, with Him we shall reign

So when they speak all manner of evil of you, hate you and mistreat you
Love them that hate you, bless them that curse you and pray for them that despitefully use you
Jesus did it, so we can too
After all, He said "greater works than these shall we do"

The Lord gives strength and the power of endurance
The word, the armor of God, His blessed assurance
With Jesus' name I can stand and you can too
It is none of your business how others treat you
Give no attention to evil, neither give place to the devil
It is your business, in the darkness to let your light shine through
Illuminating all wickedness and evil around you

The Lord has placed your feet on higher ground
Don't belittle yourself to beggarly elements of this world like a fool or a thug
You're better than that, we wrestle not against flesh and blood

But against the rulers of darkness, against the princes of the air
We battle in fasting, we battle in prayer
When it's all said and done, with Christ we'll be joint heirs

So hold fast the profession of our faith
For God is good and God is great!

Love

Love is patient, love is kind
And does not try to undermine

Love suffers long and envieth not
Love is humble though the battle is hot

Love does not vaunt itself and is not puffed up
With the love of Jesus, Lord fill our cups

Love does not behave unseemly and does not seek her own
Love is good to be spoken of, but greater when its shown

Love is not easily provoked and thinks no evil
Love is pure, love is true and in God's perfect and divine will

Love rejoiceth not in iniquity, but seeks only for good
We ought to be our brothers keeper and love them as we should

Love bears all things, endures all things
What peace, what bliss, what joy it brings
Love builds up and does not break down or destroy
True love is proven when tested, tried and employed

Love is compassionate and ready to forgive
Let love be exuded, rise up and live

Love congregates
And does not dissimilate or hate

Unfeigned, unconditional love is what Jesus gave to me
How can we say we love the invisible God if we don't love our brother who we can see

Jesus loves me this I know
For the Bible tells me so

Jesus died on the cross because of love
He left His heavenly throne and glory above

He became sin for us, who knew no sin
To give us life, joy, and peace within

God received me and loved me just as I am
It was all part of God's perfect plan

God did not call us to judge anyone
But to love with the love of Jesus, God's only begotten Son

Love thy neighbor as thyself in the love that you give
Your love will speak volumes and make a difference impacting the world in which we live

Love brings together and does not tear apart
What a better place the world would be if we all made a start
To begin to love each and everyone straight from the heart

All other things will surely vanish and fail
But the love of Jesus will always prevail

Peace

Peace in the valleys, peace in the hills
I can hear God's still small voice saying "Peace be still"

God gives peace which passeth all understanding
A peace from above that no man can give

Sweet peace have they that love the Lord
Peace which silver and gold could not afford

He is the Everlasting Father, our Prince of Peace
Trust in the Lord Jesus, and your peace He will increase

He will keep them in perfect peace, whose minds are stayed on Him
With the peace of God you will overcome and every battle you will win

Keep God's commandments and you will have peace as a river
He is well able to keep you, preserve you and deliver

Let not your heart be troubled, neither let it be
    afraid
Rest assured and receive the blessing and the promises He has made

The words that God has spoken are so you might
    have peace in Him
Be of good cheer, He has overcome the world,
    though come trials and tribulations

Seek peace and ensue it
Sometimes when things get rough, you just got to
    pursue it

We have peace with God through our Lord Jesus
    Christ
The God of peace abideth with you when you lead
    a peaceful and godly life

Prayer of Faith

Prayer changes things, you better believe
Prayer is by faith and not by what you hear or see

See the end of your prayer through the eyes of faith
All you need is a mustard seed, it's never too late

Pray non ceasing every chance you get
Push until something happens, God is not through with you yet

Pray in the good times and in the bad
Pray when you're happy and when you're sad

Prayer is not something that is based on your feelings
Or not just when you need a touch of God's healing

Prayer is all about relationship with God
The one who you worship, the one who you laud

Get to know who God is for yourself
Jesus paid it all and He removed the mighty gulf

We now have access to the throne of grace
Morning, noon and night we can seek His face

We can tell it to Jesus, our deepest hearts desires
His ears are bowed down to our prayers and He's never too tired

The Lord that keeps us never slumbers nor sleeps
Every promise He has made He surely will keep

Through prayer the impossible is made possible and barriers are broken
In every faith filled, power packed word that is spoken

From our lips to God's ears, in heaven up above
Wait on the Lord, He cares for you, He is a God of love

Prayer changes things, you better believe
Through prayer, what the heart can conceive, the heart can achieve

Serve the Lord Today

Caught betwixt two, unsure what to do
When you wish to do good, evil is present with you

Don't you know the wages of sin is death
But, walk in the spirit and you will not fulfill the lust of the flesh

Be loosed in the name of Jesus, and be ye set free
If you would only resist the devil then he would flee from thee

Greater is He that is in you, than he that is in the world
You can live, you're an over comer, let the word of God be your shield and sword

Let the Bible be your compass, ordering your steps
Perfecting you in holiness and in righteousness

God can take you from the dunghill to the mountain top
Just stand upon Jesus Christ, who is the Solid Rock

He desires to save you and give you refuge for your soul
To cleanse you and to wash you and make you every whit whole

He wants to bless you and prosper you and carry you the whole way through
If you only knew the thought that Jesus has towards you

Thoughts of good and not of evil, to give you an expected end
He came that you might have life and not to condemn

His love covers and surpasses the multitude of your sins
When you repent from a true heart, He is ready to receive you, restore you and forgive

Jesus He still loves you although you've gone astray
He will sustain you by His grace, only trust and obey

God blesses us with more than we will ever deserve
He is gracious and He's merciful, that's the God we serve

Let self be slain in subjection and give your life today
Surrender your all to Him, let go and let God have
    His way

Through trials, temptations and tribulations, things
    don't always go the way they should
But the Lord is on your side and He's working it
    out for your good

Tomorrow is not promised, so there is no time to
    waste
Come boldly to the throne of grace and daily seek
    His face

The past is now behind you, so walk in newness
    of life
And press for the mark of the high calling, which
    is in Jesus Christ

The battle is already won we have the victory
From glory to glory, He wrote your destiny

Seek ye first His righteousness and the Kingdom
And you shall have one hundred fold in this life and
    life everlasting in the life to come

The Almighty God

Lord of lords and King of kings
The almighty God Elohim

Jesus, God's beloved Son
Blessed and holy potentate one

The bread of life, the Lamb of God that was slain
Hosanna in the highest, He is worthy to be praised

He is the Good Shepherd that careth for the sheep
He is not a hireling and no, will not flee

He never leaves us nor forsakes us
He is a God we can depend on, He is a God we can trust

He is Adoni, El-Shaddi
God our Master, our Father, He is the Most High

He is the Alpha and the Omega, the beginning and the end
He sticketh closer than a brother and He's our dearest friend

He is the author and finisher of our faith, who for
  joy despised the shame
He is set down at the right hand of the throne of
  God, glory, glory to His name

He is a Wonderful Counselor, our Prince of Peace
Every burden we bear, He will release

He is Immanuel, God with us
Creator of all things, He formed man from the dust

He is Jehovah Jireh, our every need is supplied
According to His riches in glory by Christ

He is Jehovah Nissi, the Lord our banner
When the enemy comes in like a flood, the Spirit
  of the Lord will raise up a standard

He is our Messiah, our Savior, the Anointed One
Redeeming us unto Himself, from the worlds
  foundation

He is the lawgiver, judge over all
He keeps and preserves our soul, lest we fall

He is the light of the world, illuminating and dispelling the darkness
He is our rock, He is our fortress

He is our mediator as we pray
Interceding on our behalf, each and every day

He is the resurrection and the life
If we believe, we shall live and not die

He is the true vine that purgeth the branch
Through Him we have been given a second chance

God is a very present help in time of trouble, lift up thine eyes unto the hills
He is an on time God, although sometimes He may tarry, be patient and be still

So praise Him with your whole heart, mind and soul
Let the Holy Spirit take full control

Serve the Lord with gladness and you will be blessed
Laud Him and worship Him in the beauty of holiness

There is fullness of joy and pleasures in His presence
Jesus' name makes all the difference

The Year of Release

I am here to declare
I am here to decree
This is my year of release
I'm loosed, I'm delivered, I've been set free

This world and its system has nothing on me
I will prevail, I will triumph over the enemy

The devil thought he had me
And thought that I would quit

But God turned it
And worked it out to my benefit

I just lift my hands in worship
Giving glory to His name

Leaving the enemy confused
When Jesus' name I still proclaim

Be not weary in well doing
For in due season you shall reap, if you faint not

The battle is the Lord's
And not mine or yours to be fought

I am here to declare
I am here to decree
This is my year of release
I have the victory

The devil is a liar
And so are his angels too

If God be for you
Who can be against you

Every debt is paid
And every chain is broken

The blessing of the Lord is upon me
I'm engulfed in His presence and His anointing

The blood of Jesus covers me
Everywhere I go

It time to give the devil notice
And let the devil know

It's harvest time in Zion
I'm reaping what I've sown

I am here to declare
I am here to decree
This is my year of release
It's my Jubilee

I release blessings over our families, our marriages, our children
Blessing over our finances, prosperity, riches and wealth

I release blessing over our bodies
That we may have divine health

May God bless us in every faucet of our being
Mind, body and soul

And may God have His way
And the Holy Spirit take full control

May God bless us in our uprising
And in our down sitting

May there be no lack or want
But special provision

God is omniscient and knows our every need
He will supply it, if we would only worship Him
    and take heed

I am here to declare
I am here to decree
This is my year of release
I'm loosed, I'm delivered, I've been set free

This world and its system has nothing on me
I will prevail, I will triumph over the enemy

What is My Duty?

The whole duty of man is to fear God and keep His commandments
Holy and acceptable, a living sacrifice to God we present

It is my duty to be unblemished and unspotted from sin
Purified from deep within

It is my duty to come out from among them and be separate from the world
Standing faithful on God's precious holy word

It is my duty to sanctify and consecrate myself
Being heavenly minded, not lusting after earthly riches or wealth

Temporal things which vanish away
Heaven bound, steadfast and sure, never to go astray

Riches in glory should be our hearts desire
Greater heights and deeper depths to aspire

It is my duty to serve God from the heart with every fiber of my being
Behind closed doors when nobody sees

Not for vain glory or praise of men
In spirit and in truth and not for pretence

God desires truth from the inward parts
And for us to be called out and set apart

It is my duty to tell others about Jesus Christ
And that because of His love towards us, so unconditional, He sacrificed His life

It is my duty to let my light shine before men
And lead others to glorify my Father in Heaven

My duty is to give Him all the glory due to His name
To live a lifestyle of worship and praise

You Might Be the Only Jesus They See

You have an opportunity where you can help
Do you think of others or just think of yourself

Are we considering what about me
Or do we extend to our neighbor in hospitality

Ponder this thought diligently
That you might be the only Jesus they see

There was a man that fell among thieves
Do you offer assistance or just let him be

The Scribes and Pharisees they turned a blind eye
Did not offer assistance or even try

But the good Samaritan took him to the inn
And washed him, clothed him and fed him

So ponder this thought diligently
That you might be the only Jesus they see

There may be sometimes others don't treat you right
Do you treat them the way they treat you and put
    up a fight

Be wise as serpents, harmless as doves
Serve God in humility and be conscious there is our
    heavenly Father looking down from up above

We are ambassadors for Christ
To shine forth our light

Your good works all men will see
And be led to glorify our Father in the heavenlies

So ponder this thought diligently
That you might be the only Jesus they see

There's someone who is down and out
Who does not know what serving Jesus is all about

Do you offer a word of encouragement or a smile
    of cheer
And let them know that Jesus is always there

So ponder this thought diligently
That you might be the only Jesus they see

There are those who are from dysfunctional homes
And in the world they feel so all alone

Down, discouraged, feeling blue
And they need someone just like you

To uplift and build what has been broken down
Turning their situation for the better, all around

So ponder this thought diligently
That you might be the only Jesus they see

There are those who are homeless and live on the streets
Do we offer food and clothes to meet a need

Do we say in our hearts, no that's just too much
If we take a look around, we have so many stuff

Jesus said, if you have done it unto the least of these
You have also done it unto me
So ponder this thought diligently
That you might be the only Jesus they see

There are so many lost souls that need to be saved
Do you witness to others and proclaim Jesus' name

Tell them that Jesus the savior loves them and He is your all in all
They may very well take heed and be saved and answer to the call

So ponder this thought diligently
That you might be the only Jesus they see

Have you visited the sick in the hospital today
Do you believe for their healing, do you lay hands and pray

The Word of God says, the prayer of faith shall heal the sick
And His blessing, He addeth no sorrow with it

So ponder this thought diligently
That you might be the only Jesus they see

You are suddenly faced with a situation
Where telling a lie would cover your sin
Are you a person of integrity
Do you speak the truth no matter what the consequence might be

We are called to worship God in spirit and in truth
Trust God, He is able to work it out for your good

So ponder this thought diligently
That you might be the only Jesus they see

We are God's hands and feet in the world, so of faith, fight the good fight
Show forth the praises of Him who hath called you out of darkness into His marvelous light

The world is watching how Christians behave
Be true and not false, live without sin and blame

Be also an example to the believers
Serve God with excellence, be overachievers

The church must effect change in the world by the life that we live
As disciples of Christ, we need to serve, reach out, and give
So ponder this thought diligently
That you might be the only Jesus they see

About the Author

Donnalee Jemmison is a poet that has been engaged in writing poetry for the past fourteen years. She was born in Brampton Ontario, Canada, on August 19th, 1981, to parents David Jemmison and Janet Jemmison. Donnalee is an IT Professional who holds a Diploma in Network and Internet Support. In her spare time she enjoys the hobbies of exercising, reading and listening to music. Donnalee is a dedicated and devoted Christian who has a great passion and love for God and the Bible that has motivated her to write this wonderful collection of poetry, *Reaping the Harvest of God's Word,* pertaining to the word of God.